THE PRESIDENT OF DESOLATION

&

OTHER POEMS

Jerome Rothenberg

THE PRESIDENT OF DESOLATION

&

OTHER POEMS

BLACK
WIDOW
PRESS

2019

Joseph S. Phillips and Susan J. Wood, Ph.D., Publishers
www.blackwidowpress.com

Cover art: Hieronymus Bosch. *The Garden of Earthly Delights*, detail of Hell panel, 1490–1500, Grisaille, Oil on oak panel. Collection of Museo Nacional del Prado.
Cover design: Kerrie Kemperman
Book production: Kerrie Kemperman

ISBN-13: 978-0-9995803-8-7

Printed in the United States

10 9 8 7 6 5 4 3 2 1

TABLE OF CONTENTS

FURTHER AUTOVARIATIONS
Reminders of a Vanished Earth

1/
THE POEM AS LANDSCAPE

the definition
of a place
is more than
what was seen
or what was
felt before
when dreaming
of the dead
the way
a conflagration
wrapped itself
around his world
leaving in his mind
a trace of dunes
the fallout from
a ring of mountains
reminders
of a vanished earth
the landscape
marked with rising tufts
the hardness of
clay tiles

that press against
our feet like bricks
the soil concealed
beneath its coverings
through which a weave
of twisted wires
crisscross the empty
field as markers
to commemorate
the hapless dead
the ones who fly
around like ghosts
bereft of either
home or tomb
in what would once
have been their world
the count fades out
beyond 10,000
leaves them to be swept
down endless ages
fused together
or else set apart
lost nomads
on the road
to desolation
a field on mars
they wait to share
with others
dead at last

2/
NEVER DONE COUNTING

Enclosed by matter
all my thoughts
scream for prophecy.
When I wake up on Mondays
the night sky is hanging
above me   galaxies
shedding their images
fading unknown
in the half light
a light that confounds me.
Nothing we know is unreal
& nothing is real.
There is only the face
of a woman
blind in the sun
& a voice that cries out
in a language like French.
When she raises her arms
they look distant & lame,
something there
that won't work but falls flat
against me. I will follow her
up to the moon, will watch her
paint herself red
with no sense
of the distances
still to be traveled,
no plot to adjust to
but numbers
that show me

the little I know,
the way one
vanishing universe
shrinks till it swallows
another.
There are worlds here
hidden from sight
whose ends are like
their beginnings,
the world in daylight
turns dark
the blaze of noon
caught in their mirrors,
as the sun slips
through our fingers
never done counting
where the globe
has dropped
out of sight.

3/

A DEEP ROMANTIC CHASM

Head facing downward
I descend the chasm
little caring
about space or time
my face caught halfway
between dark & light
a mix of random chance
& kindred circumstances,
before I reach the bottom

& a narrow street
alongside which I spot
a darkly churning stream
& follow it
until I reach its source.

Here is a world
*outside of time & season**   *rhyme & reason
only broken by the sound
of ghostly birds
that blast us till we find
that we've arrived
nearby a field behind
a battered wooden fence,
the specters in that world
stare out at us,
move back & forth
until they cover the horizon, come
forward, forward
rising in their legions.

All they have to offer
is a turn, a word,
a sound that we can hear
& answer in return,
what has long been known
but left unspoken,
words from inner space
the tongue turns off,
the dead will learn
to speak again, the universe
is theirs & covers them
until they flee at morning,

leave us in a dream still,
faces awash with dew.

This will be the final book
the poet dreams or writes,
whose home is in his mind
or maybe elsewhere,
follows it around the world
to where it leads him,
a space forever dark
an air so heavy
that he cannot push through it
or recognize the faces
waiting for him as before
too distant to pursue,
the world once full of smiles
now dark with tears.

I am not he,
the wanderer, the captive,
the one who lives his life
as in a dream,
the messages that reach him
from a dying galaxy
fall on deaf ears,
echoes of an empty sky
the final world bereft
of sounds & images,
returned to what it was,
adrift & mindless,
the grim memento
of its absent god.

4/
TO TAKE DEATH AS A TRIBUTE
for Will Alexander

Let us step out
among the suns,
so bright the eye
sees dragons
in a panoply
of gold,
like letters
from Sumeria,
overwrought
with crazy omens
signs of our
impending death
for which they serve
as tribute
blind & held back
till they plunge
down cliffs
into the burning water
barely kept
from drowning.

In the ancient dream
a wife
is ravaged
by a lesser god
who takes the form
of a dark scorpion
the lower part
of a chimera

& tracks her
as his prey
the target of his
mad maneuverings
frenetic
with a lover's zeal
that knows
nor start nor end
no more than what
we always knew
the end as lost
as the beginning.

Always there were
footprints
on the dune
the traces
of a monster
like a god
a hidden universe
or cosmos
shining back at us
from some dark
mirror
hidden place
that might have been
a bishop's
or a king's
a trap devised
to strike & freeze
your innards
while their voices
babble

in each other's
dreams.

5/
LARGER THAN LIFE (1)

a word
escaping
from his broken
tongue
where in his bed
he lies & cries
like someone
crucified

he dreams
of distant worlds
a fabled cave
called Europe
brought to him
by messengers
crazed squads
of angels
freaky
in their feathers
children
of the sun

around their necks
each wears
a snake the more
they fly

the more
it dangles
freely

searching
for a place
to rest
they perch
on trees
& look down
where the babe
stares back
black in
the flames
looks thru
his absent eyes
his face
in shreds
the lips
half chewed

where will he find
a place
to hide from it
what days
are still to come
what games
still worth
their playing
where the names
are hidden
by their grieving
mothers buried

in a corner
of those little
minds

there is no help
for it
no sleep
or rest
left
in an empty field
or lonely
in a bed
where no one
offers up
a soothing hand

the overture
to dreams
leaves him
so restless
he searches
for his thoughts
but finds
the words
escape him
muddy-eyed
& muted

what opens
as a scream
ends in a sigh
a feckless answer
to the mystery

of time
that that which
has no start
can have
no ending
& what does have
will end
when all
is dead

for which
no testament
remains
no witness
when the witnesses
are lined behind
a broken wall
an empty sky
above
only an image
signifying
nothing

darkness
at its center
& an absent god
the residue
of what the mind
dreams
till it vanishes
both mind
& god

leaving
a pale stain
behind him

neither an omen
nor a harbinger
but the reminder
of what was once
a settled life

6/
LARGER THAN LIFE (2)

He is left
without a word
but nailed
onto his bed
like someone
crucified
he starts to dream
of Europe
in a countryside
where angels
run half-blinded
feel the power waning
from a dying sun,
long shadows form
a wall of snakes
each one a shape
that dangles
ghostlike, clambers up

a single tree
each with a face
much like a babe's
the light escaping
from their eyes
the eyelids
chewed
& cast aside
days beyond days
how many lost
while dreaming, playing
murmuring the songs
their fathers sang,
still in their minds
no time for solace
nor a moment's rest
the man locked in
the prison of his bed
from which a foot
breaks free, a hand
frantic & fierce
escapes from his,
the punishment
for angry words
let loose
no longer muted
calling forth a shudder
or a sigh
to mark the end of
space & time
nowhere to turn or hide
before the ending
when the dead

bury the dead
the road to nowhere
opens, no one
riding it but smacking up
against a wall
to die in pieces
like the image of
the battered body
of their god
hidden beneath
a bed of leaves
the ground around him
carrying the stain
that pain delivers
as a harbinger
the victory of death
against all life.

7/
A TOWN WITHOUT A NAME

the prospect of
a change of name
much worse than
fleeing from the town
where he was born
abandoning his wares
to head out on the road
one dusty morning
the summer wind
hot on his back

into a world of nights
where no one sleeps
the pressure at his temples
leaves him numb
he stumbles past
kicks off his hat & coat
into a hall where strangers
slowly disembark
the last survivors
gathered in their final refuge

doors & windows
open, missiles flying
men with knives who taunt
the orphans of the storm
leaving a vacant space
around a shattered table
where everything once full
stands dark & empty
the swarms of refugees
know only hunger

the forgotten tastes
of home & meat
now far away, now wiping out
the hope & splendor
of a life lived
with an open hand
now that they wait for us
in ragged rows
taking the shape & size
of common laborers

whose search no sooner done
is fast forgotten
children without faces
fleeing from the little towns
their bodies battered
by a hostile wind
heavy with the smells
& purple shades of *bella-*
donna   just enough
to carry in your dreams

to know that what was once
alive is now degraded
separated from the promise
& fulfillment of divine *lavoro*
where a swarm of walkers
enough to fill your thoughts
has wandered halfway
between earth & heaven
these are what we wished for
these the long awaited

huddled masses calling us
to come to them
for whom there is no joy
no memory of peace
forgotten   lost
forever   sought
until the end arrives
& finds us* there   * binds us
at which the strangers
laugh & point

they leave us at the mercy
of a one-armed gangster
a man with anger
in his heart   a gun
he loads & holds
against your ear
leaving you to cry
before he pulls away
the world between you
overrun with silence

terror of the homeless
that the time provokes

8/

THE SLEEP OF REASON

those who are lost
& show no sign
of following the light
the feeble glowing
always up ahead
or just below the surface
makes their light turn dark
the dark turn white
preliminary to what he calls
the sleep of reason
that no matter where
he turns the monsters
are a step ahead
they catch him in his chair
with hammer blows

that leave him slumped
& open   little man
his tongue outside his mouth
who gestures without arms
the flailing in his mind persists
enough to overturn the table
where he sits & dreams
the goods of life he throws aside
looking ahead to what was lost
the future & the past lie open
knowing each word he speaks
may be the last   expelled exposed
the change of fortune
makes him shudder, drawing nigh
it overtakes the stranger
on the road   or is it him
this wistful interloper
to whom he lends an ear
the path before them circling
in the darkness twice concealed
the way it will be in the end
& was in the beginning
the eclipse of mind
that finds its twin in sleep
a place of shattered forms
the fatal flights of owls
somewhere in the frozen grass
devoid of lights & trees
they stand together timeless
under a vanished sky
the flash behind their eyes
a solitary crow or magpie
black & white & fallen

robbing the night of colors
the ravenous daytrippers   (T. Tzara)
ready to swallow
whatever escapes the mind
an exercise in random thought
leading to sleep or murder
it is for this he turns to you
ready to leave this life
his hand a salty harbinger
a blackened cup
that cannot push the time back
like a rhyme foregone
oppressive to his ears
& throwing sand into his eyes
the whole world traveled
half a foot in Spain
the rest a nightly passage
to a rotting underworld
the ceiling covered with green flies
alive & swarming
shadows casting images
the polycentric bulls
of Altamira where a hand
reached out to touch a wall
in darkness   thinking of his fate
& all he pressed against
praying for paradise
& sad to leave the world
the way he found it
the will to murder
risen raw & monstrous
the softness of his dream & yours
the patience of a rock

9/
LIKE GOD ATOP A TOWER

one in the name of science
& one of peace
the water searching for
a hole to fill
without a chance of rising
to the sky
a name so contrary
it steals your breath
your eye can barely
see it forming
words that float away
& leave you empty
no translation needed
as the father watches
& the son comes forth
his mouth alive
with light from deep inside
the skull so bright
it blinds whoever sees it
like a fire   strands of color
breaking through
he sits & watches
motionless
the tower at his back
begins to fall
so like a dog he is
his eyes half open
without a name to call him
feeling the frozen ground
a corner of his mind

reserved for ruin
for a stop to energy
& light   the empty sky
imperils a lost earth
it gives no sign of grace
no revelation of its loss
but vanishes in absence
in a world completely white
that hides all colors
feels the aftershocks
rocking the earth
that send up angry clouds
a rain of rocks & clay
enough to seal the spirit
the mind already gone
or left to chance
a time to break the line
to sweep it clean
the secrets that the mind
once knew & fled from
visions raining down
their meanings lost
turned dark & dirty
hard to comprehend
but left to circumstance
he tries to gulp it down
but falters
all is singular
& leaves no trace
other than what his speech
allows him while it hides
the contours of all he writes
& time erases

to mark the burial of thoughts
lost in a field of light
in which each particle
is there & nowhere
leaving a blank inside each eye
ready to seed with words
the more his right hand writes
his left wipes clean

10/
I HOLD DARK MATTER

matter glows
behind the thoughts
that hide it
prophecy so fierce
it makes a hash
of Monday
as you ride to work
the clock alarming
with its certain voice
the galaxies
above your head
in motion
hanging by
a thread
an image neither deep
nor shallow
just enough to know
what light brings forth
or hides   a mystery
compounded

& confounded
real & unreal
where the sun
reveals herself
a woman   cries
in silence
holding in her arms
the babe her son
le fils in French
like Oedipus lame-footed
if the magic works
the mother's flesh
against him
& the moon his father
a red spoiler
watches at a distance
as the plot unwinds
the numbers grow
unchecked untold
to form a universe
another place to roam
& dream   the end
still lost to sight
as what it always was
& now begins again
dark matter
staring back at you
an empty mirror
fingers slipping from
your grip
the more you count
the more they drop from you
scattered by time

11/
I FEEL THE SAND BETWEEN MY TEETH

brittle like teeth
the mouth can't hold
but take the shape
of tiny arrows
what the wolf in dreams
spews out   a cry
more like a tapping sound
like pebbles in a brook

the rat-a-tat
a wash board makes
against your fingers
or like castanets
the click & clack
precisely sand
pressed in your mouth
your tongue & teeth

feeling the grit
the particles in motion
bit after bit
you cough them up
or spit them out
leaving a mark on canvas
filled with blood & leaves
as many grains as stars

signaling the news
from space   the dark world
filled with signals

more than the mind
can hold   like dreams
that capture us
making a lie of time
where time runs wild

never to find
its equal
in the worlds below
through which you fall
& still will follow
absent your voice
that stays behind
silent as theirs

the black worlds opening
 to let the stars sing
from unbounded space
more like a scream
than what we cling to
rhyme & reason
stripped from us
the days ahead

turned backwards
where a river ran
& houses on the shore
were ringed by bears
encounters
endless trials & woes
we ran from
would not find an equal

in the time we knew
the end of politics
as farce & tragedy
foretold & fatal
where the naked ape
sets forth again
the power in his finger
pointing at the sky

the hidden universe & things
beyond his knowing
soon reduced to worms
a sky where stars
are also worms
the words pronounced
in foreign tongues
sounds like *gusanos*

waiting watching
with the others
& myself
among them
eyes obscured
by moonlight
without time
to think

or find a place
that saves us
from the dark
the light
the nameless killers

aiming to embark
& claim
their prize

12/
YOU WILL NOT ESCAPE

escape is too precious
too often tried
& flaunted by the killers
running from the scene

their innocence in play
a clash of words & gestures
while around you
crowds arise & vanish

juices once unleashed
flow from each orifice
your body jellied
melted in a dream

gauze cannot cover
or conceal
the empire of bone & flesh
shuttered & shattered

slippers on swollen feet
a rag atop your head
bare skin torn loose
& flapping sadly in the light

enticements for the killers
ready for the mark
their grinning faces
cold behind the glass

some will proclaim the word
against all odds
others can only wait
& wonder

bat wings brush the air
the lonely messengers
lazy in flight
what dreams are made of

& the mother still can't see
the veiled intruders
strangers in her mirror
blotting out the sun

their monkey faces
peering out
jackets stretched down
beneath their knees

shoes for the naked ape
the dew-eyed wanderer
who trades his life
for lifeless baubles

laziness in how he walks
& talks   the way

he turns the fairest of days
into the darkest

to tell it & to lose it
like the reluctant bride
her bridegroom hovering
above   sustaining her

duendes running wild
to every side of them
who leap & show their shadows
frozen in time

the air is filled with them
backwards & forwards
buoyed by burning currents
absent memories or hope

a whirlwind of dead leaves
of lives lost in its trail
stupid to even think of
though the thoughts remain

the cries are all we know
of them   of us
of her   the mind still holds
but sees them vanishing

they swing & cover
the red sky
between them nothing
worth the ride

where it becomes a path
back to the earth
the dolls in their battalions
row upon row

caprichos of earth & sky
forever broken
frail before your eyes
the token of a dream

13/
I WRITE MY NAME ON AIR

what's in a name
& what is not
but holds it on
his tongue
unspoken
till the tongue
grows numb

he dances past
with rattles
not for dreaming*   * drumming
but to speak
to drum the news
of where he dwells
the other side
of what he dreams

to tell it to the world
& let god hear you

little man who coughs
who brays*   * who prays
less from reason
than from impulse
waiting for the god
to call his name

his is the final word
the deepest wish
that grace still tries*   * flies
to reach the sacred
knowing little else
but that the sacred pains
when summoned
sharp as spurs   * as burrs

an angry father
sides with providence
against his sons
derides the mothers
women lost to time
like tethered cows
the weather changing
to a sudden wind   * a southern wind

a blue rain
covering the streets
on which I walk
between blue houses
conjuring a lady
with blue fingers
who will drive a blue comb
thru her ash blue hair

blue against the odds
she counts the house
& greets the fathers
summoned to her "show"
but steady in blue light
that lets a red man
bow down from the waist
& tip a terrible top hat

in our direction
where the darkness grows
the past returns
& overflows the margins
running to escape
we leave the world behind
no place for shame
no time for gratitude

we face our limits
and with him we bow
the clouds are blue
& red like ribbons
they fill the air
with names & cries
no way to spare our lives
or go forth gaily

14/
A CITY WITHOUT PEOPLE

to build a city
is a task

worth taking
leaving space
where people
hide, where
visitors
run wild
whose footprints
in the grit
lining
our streets
lead us astray
no sooner
counted
than the way
to death
opens before us
like a lover's
smile
his teeth
still in his skull
who peers out
pale & sightless
who has little
faith or hope
but stands above
a crumbling hill
forever lost
a stranger
to his mind
& body
while the sky turns
blue & red
he swings around

in shrinking circles
hears the cries below
of people fleeing
lost to time
more dead
than living
petals on a wet
black bough
who gather
tribes of ghosts
to trade off
what they save
in tattered photos
where the dead
stay dead
the gates half shut
half open
water pouring from
a thousand jets
they fight off with
a thousand hands
feeling the force
the angry pressure
of their backs
against a wall
from which the pediments
totter & drop
endangered life
buried beneath
an air of dust
& ashes
leaving the old
destructive element

cold & dark
nowhere a way
to break free
from the bind
we're born with
swollen in the womb
each one a ghost
or angel
where the day ends
& the night
is all that's left
alone adrift
like faceless* friends   * faithless
we learn to walk
anew but finding
little solace
even still less
in dreams

15/
OUR COMMON FATE

the cars
in dreams
are like
the cars
awake

their motion
cuts across
our table

where their wheels
leave marks

our eyes
too blank
to register
our common
fate

the human
cursed by
the divine
falls in a heap
of shadows

doling out
allotments
where the case
is shut
& open

on the boulevard
in pairs
we kneel behind
a door
sealing our thoughts

the time to shift
has passed
we cross
our legs
& stay in place

between short
bursts of air
the old world
plays a march
that calls us

unheard melodies
are more
than we can bear
so close at hand
so feral

little figures
on a board
prepared to move
a stronger force
propels us

our option is
the deeper world
to glimpse
the cosmos
through a pin hole

horses cover
every cranny
thrashing
through a sea
of stars

from which a friend
returns to life
delivers

a cold portion
scarcely felt

our minds fill up
with rhymes
& measures
hearts adrift
in endless space

a blind infinity
absent a shore

16/
A DARKNESS VISIBLE BEFORE THEIR EYES

the poem returns & finds
a fire burning angrily
around the children's graves

wide open   waiting
for the living souls
to fill them

in a rain of ashes
sand & gritty particles
driving the mind to pity

a sea of molten gold
so hot it leaves
the skin in shreds

as barren as their cities
the rattling of a door
a harbinger of rain

to cloak the lost
& fallen bodies
with small hope of rest

the blood too thick
around them muddying
their days & nights

a darkness visible
before their eyes
still darker darkness

striking the air
with sticks & digging
through the sand

the grit cracking
their teeth   no space
no place to hide

the future buried
with their skin
the day becoming night

I let the fire rise
inside your house
& mine together

giving ourselves
to death   our ashes
under a pine tree

birds over everything
slide down our chimney
cracking their wings

black morning milk
the poem of the fire-raisers
loud in my ears

the smoke never ending
dead bodies falling & flailing
their arms torn away

no longer upraised
or ascending
the last man alive

skin on fire
fire on fire
a black sun

never at rest
trapped between
body & mind

shining thru

17/
A MAN IN LOVE WITH DEATH (1)

the proof is in
the barely heard
the human lie
stuck in their throats
night covering
their faces

like a screen
an empty mirror
losing sight of what
was never theirs
an episode
out of some faded film

more empty
every time we pass
the king of their imaginations
dead & gone
his throne
a stack of blighted books

the minds of those
who squat there
a prey to forms of worship
best deferred
certain to end
in farce or frenzy

before or after
what the future holds

a round of voices
the mind can barely hear
the loss of comprehension
as another fact

a lie told to enmesh us
in his dance
right before us
still not understood
we bury with
our memories & dreams

nothing more real
than where we stand
wind in our faces
easy to forget
or to return to what
we never knew

a game played
with the hapless dead
still helpless
still escaping
what the others
see & run from

a memory
best cast aside
to struggle for
the source eluding us
his world mistaken
for our own

till everything
is brought to ruin
a fearful paradise
kept from the living
the dead left
to embrace the dead

18/
A MAN IN LOVE WITH DEATH (2)

I will figure the time of my death by inches, moving closer every chance it gets, for which denial is no longer proof.

Better to be a stone than be a man, he says, when all the others, whether near or far away, follow the same path to nowhere, bound by the last particle of breath that keeps them human.

In this way he opens up a vein & lets it bleed, a color different from the blood of closure, yellow when the light breaks through, unfiltered, purple in the night.

This is what he sees, the paradox of vision, colors on a screen that hides a screen.

Therefore to turn from it, to go back to what the eye remembers, the journey that begins in hyperspace, travels with the force of crazed computers, the end of time in sight.

No further thought, no final episode, but all that was still is.

For this no need for space flights, for escapes by opening a door & waiting for the sky to break apart, galactic winds to sweep you up & take you to a world undreamed & ever empty.

It is there I enter nightly or as the day allows, a prince of filthy propositions, bravos from the churl who would be king.

He is no better than the rest of you, waits to come into the empty room, to let the others wonder while he ponders where to sit, the darkness blanketing his spangled throne.

Hear o Israel is not a passing thought but prongs him in his deepest mind.

Untold, unthought, unwanted: where is a boy to go when life is everywhere at once, simple at first, then shaped into a trillion fleeting forms?

The universe for sure must hold enough to keep us spinning, sovereign in its mysteries that know no end.

Which brings us to the very far, away from us & gone, not here, not now, with no before or after.

The dead are who they are, remain still present when we think of them as voices sounding in the room behind us.

Never to mark a new beginning, rather to await an end & push for just a spark of comprehension.

If there is strength in numbers, then, how does it help to multiply the voices that besiege us even now, the defenders of a truth that hides a lie inside it.

Closing in from every side, whatever comes into his mind is where the truth lies, what he learns without a thought to nurture or to set it right.

Hands off is not like hands up, though they wouldn't know it, would they, running where the voices lead & bury them.

That makes some form of satisfaction, that the present ends before it starts, followed by another present, then another no more real.

There is no right or left here, all directions changing as we come at them, no one to clear the path for us, the fathers swallowed by a cosmic wind.

On their flesh the numbers burn, a sure reminder of the world that made us & now waits in silence for the sure return.

That we can keep the end in mind is fate, that we can think beyond it is a further twist, still not enough to change the game.

For which the grim computer beckons, sending messages we cannot read, enough to know the deeper world is dark, the lives it swallows helpless.

And yet they live on borrowed time, as he does when he dreams of death, no doors to let him out or let the others in.

The others are the final test, their breath a distant sound now, the fading trace of memory.

Is there a pause then, the doors shut tight against intruders & the mind returning to its silent source?

Theirs is a voice without a voice, a life without a life, a light without a light, a dream without a dream, a sky without a sky, a world without a world.

The more the voice retreats into itself the more he finds himself astonished, knowing only there is nothing left to know, or everything.

He is a man in love with death & welcomes his return to paradise, a place where no one speaks & no one stops to listen or to turn aside.

Thereby no one is lonely where all mind is no mind & no mind is all that is.

A last ambition lost: to spend eternity among the hapless dead.

NOTE. In the 1990s I composed a series of thirty-three "Lorca Variations," drawing vocabulary, principally nouns, from my previously published translation of Federico García Lorca's early gathering of poems, *The Suites*. I later made use of this method of composition for homages to Jackson Mac Low, Octavio Paz, Arshile Gorky, & others as a step beyond translation but with an idea of translation – or what Haroldo de Campos called "transcreation" & I called "othering" – as one of the defining characteristics of poetry as a whole. In the first years of the present century I drew on this method to compose & publish a new series of poems — "autovariations" — in which I used vocabulary from earlier poems of my own as I had with those of others in the previous variations. What I had in mind also were Henri Matisse's words to Gino Severini spoken a hundred years before:

> *One should be able to rework an old work at least once—to make sure that one has not fallen victim—to one's nerves or to fate.*

And again:

> *When you have achieved what you want in a certain area, when you have exploited the possibilities that lie in one direction, you must, when the time comes, change course, search for something new.*

The present Autovariations and other poems in this book bring that experiment to a virtual conclusion—unless they don't.

THE DISASTERS OF WAR
after Goya

*He is a real man
when he murders,
is he not?*

1/

*Sad presentiments
of what must come*

to pass   a rage
of shredded clothes

the darkness
through which images
rain down
a ruined world

of bricks & walls
erased   or crumbled
shattered*   * splattered
on the broken ground

made present
by an unseen hand
like mine
the lines concealing

men & women
children
trees & gardens
grass gates gravestones

shrines & temples
class rooms
radios & books
old dresses

fifes & fiddles
heirlooms
bicycles
eyeglasses

sidewalks
monuments
engagements
marriages

employees
clocks & watches
street signs
works of art

the man's face
shows it
chest & forearms
swollen

stumps for legs
the cry of blood
so fierce
it stops his heart

his eyes see only
lines like knives
criss-crossing
blood or rain

the word is misery
that binds him*   *blinds him
where the waters rush
& rage

with reason
or without
the fate of *real* men
facing off
guns at the quick
or lances

silently
the cries rise up
between clenched lips
the itch & thrill
of suffocation
driving them on

for which the mind
is never still
but races screaming

somewhere beyond
the zone
where *real* men go

theirs is the dream
of children
& old mothers
huddled masses
at their feet
the dream of where we go

& where the bayonet
enters the sad flesh
the dark device
explodes behind us
ready like them
to make its mark

the blood is like
a ribbon
where it leaves
his mouth
the knife his hand holds
hot to strike

the mind of Goya
falters   sightless
writing in a room
without a light
he feels the thrust
much like his own

the speed of thought
where thought ends
the rest is flights
of spirits
dibbiks who will never
find a home

how heavy
we have all become
trying to free our hands
to etch our names
still mindful that the dead
will never sleep

3/

the same thing
from the ax

as from the sword
the fury*   *vengeance
of the dead
against the quick

.

those who survive
remember
knives like lights
cutting through time
& leaving us
minus a hole to hide

.

swept into death
the boots
the men wear
when the feet
stop moving
stick out of the ground

.

beyond our sight
the earth
will swallow them
no hand upraised
to hold it back
or free us

.

if my hand
would thrust a knife
like yours
the blow would sever

head from throat
spreading the blood
.

down mirrors
it will flow
& when they cry
for sunlight
nothing
will answer

but the deadman's
song

4 /

the women give them
courage   seated
on the ground

the carnage
in the little world
around them
who we are
& where we go
still hidden
where their memories
are darkest
barely known

the one who lies there
with an arm
upraised
his mouth agape
where soon
the worms will enter

& the other woman
struggling
with her grim assailant
he whose hand
tugs at her hair
ready & ripe to kill

the fate of *real* men
that undoes these women
they are forever
lost to time
unable to rekindle*   *unsaddle
those who ride them

the babe at center
of the struggle
where *the women*
like wild beasts
(he says)
strike back with
sticks & stones

eyes up to heaven
from the earth
on which she lies
remembrance of a life
long gone
now seeps through
half her mind

the missing half
knows that the hand
that holds the knife
carries the power
men & animals
possess   replacements
for their measly teeth

theirs is the women's
war   at last
a solitary rifle
waiting to explode
aimed at the surrounding
emptiness   the mystery
of men & women

locked in battle
helpless to break free

6/

the lesson when all lives
are spent   the well deserved
& those less hopeful
taken by surprise
their breath suspended

whom we would join
in sleep
the bright defenders
carrying their light
into the darkest midnight

ghosts, step forth
arisen from your bodies
headless   trunkless
where the sky turns black
the sun eclipsed & lost

a spark of vengeance
trapped   deep in your blood
your bodies fast reduced
to bones & ash
the loneliness of men

who kill for pleasure
will not let it pass
but wait in silent clusters
children of the earth
that lies* beneath them   * that dies

Qué valor (cries Goya)
his eye like yours
scanning the silent bodies
dreaming of a woman
solitary   wed to death

a single hill in sight
the rest whatever
dreams can bring the dreamer
nothing more to say
our looks turned inward

where the sky is white
or vanishes
& leaves a glow behind
a spark to set
the world aflame

repeated across centuries
her foot atop
the quickly rotting
corpse   how innocent
& deadly

it becomes
how manly
in the aftermath
for which we wait
like beggars

heroes who perpetuate
the lie of war
no worse for those
who do it out of love
no better

8/

much as it always
happens
in the years before
the judgment
when the cries of men
& horses
raise the dead

my dream is yours
then   even now
it's in the way they fall
the way the rider
rises from the pile
his head capped
like a guard in dreams

a simple calculus
a calculation
how the ghosts of horses
& the ghosts of men
lie down together
nothing ever lost
but changing into air

an old horse rotting
in the open field
becomes a horse
no longer   's now
a source of light
the bristles in a blaze
harrowing the day

that follows   opens
on another day
the day beyond
waiting for the thrust
the hidden charge
so like the clamor*   *the glamour
of the days before

9/

they do not want to
but the time
is always perfect
beckons them with secret
passageways
the better to absorb
the shocks of life

the hands & handles
of the barbered man
his hat down almost
to his eyes   his body
cock thrust forward
up against her own
so eager to command

he cannot see the one
behind him   face a mask
the cloth around the body
(man or crone)
with knife raised high
about to strike
& take him down

behind them
a large wheel
like a carnival's
is turning
he would bring
his bride to
let her hang there

helpless
hapless
thoughtless
senseless
heartless
witless
nameless

until the life
escapes from them
their worlds
dissolving
carries them along

then lets them go

10/

the way is hard
& when they pull him
from the rack
the ladder shakes
beneath him

in a world of ladders
little men
breathing through
their gums
pay a tall price

the monk's voice
from the side
still preaching
showering the air
with death

or dreams
of death
to spare the ones
who ease
the dead man down

another swinging
from a plank
ascending
sorrows of the cross
flush in his ears

no light for these
their eyes shut tight
hands bound
or clenched in prayer
& suffering

for Goya too
the pain starts

first in his hands
like theirs
then in his eyes

the images
on fire
like a thousand suns
will end in
darkness

lost to
sight & sound
his body soon
will sail into the air
& vanish

11/

and it can't be helped
however hard they push
leaving the field
to those who can
no longer see
or cry

example of the man
bound to a stake
the mask over his eyes
pulled tight
enough to blind him
in the sight of god

face looking down
a face no longer
at his feet
the shattered body
eyeless
on the bloody earth

the massacre won't end
the carnage grows
behind him
real men aim their guns
the bodies of the dying
tied & falling

no one can escape
but war will find them all
poor hirelings & slaves

the reckoning won't end
the call to arms
once halted   sounds again

across the centuries
earth unmindful
of the fate of millions
from the smallest death
to what grows fat
& can't be counted

12/

how he defends himself
the best he can
poor nag among

the pack of others
son of sorrow
without hope of home

too many sounds
surround him
too much debris
it only takes
the saddest remnant
to upend the best

the two of us
lost souls
hearing the cries of hounds
the pressures of the pack
leaving no space
to breathe

the life of dogs
surrounds us
those who wait
to pounce   to bring
their quarry
down to earth

the dogs of war
signal the charge
the dark days
trap us all
spectators to a race
no one can win

they take advantage
of what they find
& thrive on it
bare bodies stripped
flayed to the bone

ever afraid
the dead could wake
lonely & cold
the hungry phantoms
ready to strike back

in dreams they see
the clothes resisting
feel the bodies
stiffening
electric to the touch

it makes them freeze
the hard ground
darkening with blood
I watch & swoon
along with Goya

we are hand in hand
both blind & trembling
centuries & deaths
careening past us
standing dazed

amazed to name
the new disasters
always more
& always crueler
than the days before

14/

they do not agree
or do they?
even now they watch
as we do
images of power
in the captain's mind

a line of blades
over the broken bodies
the mad lieutenant
signaling the charge
eager for the carnage
that the night allows

the ambivalence
of those who kill
murderers & men
dressed for the night*   * the fight
who kiss & run
kiss & run amok

a stranger in
a crushed hat
knows the way
his dark face
staring back at us
hands tied

& the ones
you first imagined
wait here too
killers to the end
their glee is rank
& perfect

never to be tamed
they crack your mind
& enter   horses
nuzzling horses
killers bending down
to brush the lips

the fingertips
of killers
hand in hand
brought back to life
now & forever
eager to leap forward

killing those
who are not them

15/

enough to bury them
& keeping quiet
to move on
the way that time
extends
from life to life

a new page from
the book of witness
dropping from the sky
or in a rage
the earth exploding
where they walk

little by little
foot by foot
the ones who take
our measure
never change
nor do the bodies

whether viewed
across the field
or from the distant sky
once teeming
strewn with angry gods
now drones

the stink of death
both near & far
the grieving couple
separated   set aside

their silent cries
across the centuries

the cruel minions
vanished
only the open grave
remaining open
where the skin will turn
to dirt

the bones to bones
a taste of history
waiting to be unearthed
& counted
never more real
than now

16/

there is no time left
in the end   no sunlight
where a sword or gun
can tear apart
what hope remains

the force of arms so strong
it overrides them
waiting for the final kill
the thrill of terror
that the victim leaves us

everyone who dreams
dreams hard
pretending it doesn't change
the interlopers
push against a wall

like real men
on the hunt
for death & pleasure
bringing them
to ground

the bodies
starting to pile up
once & again
sex hotter
in the face of death

how can it be
more real than this

whether belief or what
their angry prongs
pursue

that makes us
look back
where we see
ourselves
in broken mirrors

killers & victims both
the cruelty & cries
of the forsaken
disasters of a war
without a start or end

17/

all this & more
the arch assassins

lay out the bodies
in the stiffness
death demands

from one & all
the count repeated
over centuries
from his time
to mine

real men splayed out
stacked up against
each other
war's unburied
children

the word is *slaughter*
false reports
& real
the value of the seen
now overwhelms us

glimpsed from above
as now the present time
allows us   & the terror
also from above
masking a hostile sky

but Goya's bodies
say enough
the blood smeared
on the weapon
that the dead man holds

a blur of empty houses
blasted brought to dust
unbarred unhinged
dissolving slowly
in a frozen dream

& the mound behind
the start of what
will be a single grave
for all to lie in
newly awakened in the mind

the sound of war
fades out
for those who lie there
while the others wait
their time already nigh

18/

the same thing
everywhere you look
they lie face down
a carpet cut
to cover them
in death

a scissor
out of their reach
lies cast aside
discarded
after the deed
is done

my own blood
ready to seep out
like honey
soles of shoes
worn thin
the soul set free

out of a hole
torn in the dead man's
chest   escaped
from life
& what the slaughtered
leave for us

the artist's eye
ends in a wall
a cavern opening

on clouds & light
more heaps of bodies
in the open air

no inch of ground
without its bodies
what if anything to say
dear Goya?
gliding through your dream
we rise & fall

19/

the consequences,
high above
the fallen body,

where a swarm of bats
swoops down

the master bat,
a man's size
tearing at his shirt
to reach the flesh
your dream lets in

bat crazy after war
the dead man
resting on a carpet
of his blood
can't face us

hippodromes race
from his mind
& magic cries
leaving an empty
space within

the transformations
start   unfettered
where the master bat
becomes an owl
while a cat looks on

perched on an altar
while the *feline pantomime*
takes shape
a monk in prayer
completes the scene

no one a master
more than you
who frames
those images
the war long gone

the bat & cat
making a perfect rhyme
like mud & blood
a man can bow before
absent their god

watched by a single
shade where once
a throng held sway
my mind evades it too
too much to bear

I wait to hear him
hooded man who prays
& stops
prays & stops again
untongued

I lick my fingers
dreaming that the war
is done but knowing
that it waits inside us
ready to implode

20/

El buitre carnivoro.

hungry for blood
the fabled vulture
doth ascend,

the soldier
with a pitchfork
smites him hard

mocking the cry
of empire
the scream inside
the deaf man's ear
how many fall
under his sway

like phantoms
risen from
your dreams
the refugees
who run & founder
rise & fall

again   aghast
those whom the war
has left behind
whose cries
the deaf man
cannot hear

only the fog of war
the dull drone
of his own voice now
over the stricken throng
a monotone of nasals
hollowed out

no time   no space
the rage for beauty
stricken from
the vulture's mind
towering above
his vanished world

the mind of Goya
is his mind
no longer   even here
the distance
acts against him
blurs his footfall

where he stumbles
poor old bird
knowing that the time
draws nigh
when sound & sight
no longer matter

feathered arms
imperious but hapless
death the master
as he is for all
a paradise of bodies
& a silent hell

truth dies
faster
than the blur
of faces
goggled men

& broken bodies
wrapped inside
the shadows
each one casts
a lie that traps them

while the bride
lies flayed
the scraps left
that the mind, eroded,
cannot grasp

those who have died
for nothing
die for truth
no longer
but construct their own

for which some weep*   * some sweep
some hold a broom
or rake   to scrape
the ground around her
daughter of the dust

hardly aware that over her
the dark deceiver hovers
keeper of a lie
that leaves her pinned
& helpless

at a time when lies
again take over
that the mind eroded
cannot see
but holds as true

this is his time
& ours
the lie triumphant
triggers our belief
& lets it die

as she does

AT THE HOTEL MONOPOL
in Breslau

PROEM. [1988] *It was raining when we got to Wrocław, the miles from Auschwitz bringing back the memories of what had happened there. Traveling with our son we had made reservations for a single suite at the Hotel Monopol, but when we pulled in, the hotel could only come up with two separate rooms. After a while, though, the desk clerk said that they had found a suite for us that was free. An elderly bellhop carried our bags up the central flight of stairs, threw the big doors open, put our bags down on the floor, & asked me with a little smile, "And do you know who slept here?" Then he answered his own question: "Hitler!—And he made a speech from that balcony." After which he turned & closed the doors behind him, leaving us to think again about our fate & theirs.*

in the room
where Hitler slept
dreams didn't come
but sounds
broke from the walls

& cracked
then crackled
made us stare down
past our feet
the dance beginning

while over our heads
the lights would flicker
one-two-three-four
brought to life
we stepped out

on his balcony
& hailed the crowds
hard faces
four-two-three-one
theirs like ours

our fingers flat
above our lips
looking like hairs   [two fingers held above his lip]
bunched up
touched by his tongue

the rain falls
upside-down
from iron boxes
the dead outside the ring
surround us

cousins fallen
bird-eyed
where the rain

like tiny knives
opens their wounds

children & rain
the redfaced killers
reach up to the man
the victims without faces
broken underfoot

four-one-three-two
I hadn't been there
where the lines of gymnasts
march to the sounds
of open flesh

for them his face
is golden
old as time & echoing
the cry of what can never
be reborn

2/
the other century
still fills the air
with sounds & colors
fills my mouth
with half-chewed words

long past the time
to get it written
what returns at night
is the reprise
of total death

with not a stone
unturned   unthrown
the bodies dropped
like logs
into a global pit*   * a hole of shit

from & thru which
little deaths run wild
the bones imploding*   * eroding
in his throat
to feed his pleasures

Dante no less cruel
than Bosch
the cries of fancy
silencing the caged
imagination

turn the killer
upside down
& from his mouth
the burning babes
will drop

the distance
between life & death
reduced to silence
like a world*   * a word
in cyber space

birds come to life
& scatter*   *shatter
where the dead

reach for the dead
but lose all touch

what ugliness
unleashed & rising
where we sleep
open to the times*   * the rhymes
the hells he leaves us

3/
to enter
like fools
into the killer's
dark dance
feet on marbled floors
& still alive

I want to sound it
pounding on the walls
to hear my voice
like his
bounce back to me
time beyond time

was how we danced there
pranced & ranted
to the open air
then fell into the bed
from which his ghost
blew empty words

the hapless dead
were with us

auschwitz only miles away
treblinka coughed them up
the cousins sundered
by the killer's whims

their faces weren't
faces   more like
masks & masqueraders
mysteries we carry
scratched into the heart
& mind

the mouth falls open
laughter breaks
the spell   the children
dance with us
& die
the dream* won't end   * the scream

4/
who are the others
here   what others
join the dance
the hoky-poky dancers
primed to kill

across the century
their dance won't end
but follows us
from room to room*   *from tomb to tomb
& back again

a manga world
the hated faces crammed
into a child's mind
never to be erased
but slowly magnified

how many arms
are raised   how many
mouths engulf
the burning babe
wiping the spit away

the fires rage
again   again
the legions promenade
they watch his pale hand
rise & fall

Savonarola's burning

THE POUND PROJECT

Swollen-eyed, rested,
        lids sinking, darkness unconscious

....

And before hell mouth; dry plain
and two mountains

1/
head down,
screwed into the swill

I am led into a home
where no one
– not a dog or cat –
drops by.

The body of a
strangled child

stares out
& spooks me.

Warriors & children
fill my eyes.

2/
A lady asks me.
I speak in season.

With my old
suburban voice
my prejudice
grows ripe.

I am not empty
but without a taste
for differences
I atrophy.

The dance gets harder
as the mud gets high.

3/
I mate with my free kind
upon the crags.

I neither wait for you
nor need you,
feel the pressure of your tongue
that calls me down.

I know extremis
better than the cackling
of my fellows,
gaunt & green with pain.

In my hand a flower
blossoms, does it not?

4/
I let down the crystal curtain
& watch the moon.

Men & animals surround me,
I am led by these
into a hole, brown-colored
like my arm.

I wait for words the night
once brought me,
luminous, the sky a changing
field of light.

While here below,
        their sightless eyes
confound me.

5/
Nor can I shift my pains
to other,

much less my words
high on your wall.
that face me down
an afterthought
to careless speech.

We teach forgiveness
to the idle only.
For the rest the suffering
leaves its own mark.

You back away from mine,
old face like yours.

6/
I am the help of the aged;
I pay men to talk peace.

With my hands I raise
a sagging body.   I am keen
& run before them,
meaning to escape.

I pay a price for
bounty. Deaf
I hear a call
to war.

Somewhere within me
armies clash.

7/
I have weathered the storm,
I have beaten out my exile.

I have made a pact with someone
& have botched it. Freed from time
my fingers have grown frail,
my pen lies helpless on the floor.

I have desires that my flesh
still harbors. Little help or gratitude
will come from those
my turnings have betrayed.

I watch the dead file by
& feel a stirring.

8/
singing: O sweet and lovely
o Lady be good

the song is traveling
from my time into yours,
like Ella's song, is
wordless.

Hear me sing it   see me
dance on water.
I coast down the street
the while my eyes

like everyman's eyes
     fill with apparitions
a *dead bullock.*

9/
Blown around the feet of
the God,

the landscape hides from us,
the little castle
shows its face at night
& shamans walk the streets

communing with the dead
the terror of the folk
in agony   the cries
of those who fled to open water

gathered into caves
who took their lives.

Okinawa 1945/2000

10/
Where the dead walked
   And the living were made of cardboard
their shadows disappeared.

I lost track of eternity
that makes things new.

Nothing here improves
while time is lost.

Clean as any whistle
I come forth.

But still I can't shake off
the memory of mud.

In meiner heimat.

11/
"I am noman,
my name is noman"

I wait where road
crosses road,
where hunters fly from
their quarry.

Not me but those
that I point to!
Not those but the dead
fed with blood!

Their hands rise in fury.
They hammer us down.

12/
The yidd is a stimulant
and the goyim are cattle

& the words once written
stay writ   all his words
coming back to the speaker
laying him flat.

What a downfall I had
& what havens I reached for
too late. None remained
to embrace me, but

jews, real jews, not shades
in my head but avengers.

13/
First must thou go
the road to hell

must see the millions
thou hast smitten
with thy thoughts   must cry
the cry of killers.

If thy hands are clean
as mine are
why then the swelling in thy throat
the smells of vomit?

Blinded as the dead are blind
the kings of hell.

14/
Time is the evil.
Evil.

Is what is always lost,
what takes me by the throat
& leaves me, shrunken
begging with the other thieves

then drops me in the pit
called bolgia, where a
rhyme I can't erase
repeats forever.

For others other pits
shadow their lives.

15/
the soil living pus, full of vermin,
dead maggots begetting live maggots

fascists at banquets,
pandars to authority,
jackboots,
skinheads with iron teeth

sucking hard at our flesh,
shoving old men
like books in their fires,
outcroppings of shit

too raw for feeling,
the flux in the corpse
turns to stone.

16/
And I am not a demigod,
I cannot make it cohere.

Nor bring it, at a dare,
into my focus,
where the sunlight even now
turns ashen,

heavy with burnt matter,
stinking, where the century
has turned a corner,
like a swollen foetus

it has pulled me down,
          old vanity
has pulled me down.

NOTE. "The Pound Project" was commissioned by Francesco Conz for a verbal-visual
project in association with Mary de Rachewiltz & the Pound estate at Schloss Brunne-
burg in the Tirol. The various artists & poets in the project were each responsible for a
suite of sixteen works responsive to aspects of Pound's own life & writings. In my case
the sixteen poems included appropriations of lines from Pound – shown here in italics –
& a sense of his voice & mine mingling without (so to speak) rime or reason. There was
also a visual component, a photo image of Pound's face, variously collaged & colored,
but I have chosen not to show it here, rather to borrow the three-fold photo image,
above, collaged & further modified, after Richard Avedon.

AMERICA/2018
The President of Desolation

1/
that farce
replaces tragedy
obscene
even to think it

& yet to come
into another age
& find it
proven true

this is the price of
growing old
the progress truly
of a state

of mind
America
the center
both

of mind
the gap
& mindless
space

2/
not farce but madness
from the start
the roots of tragedy
embedded
in the barely human
ready to bring us down

to which he leads us
in a dream
almost as deadly
as a tunnel
the mind winds through
seeing the sky ahead

but kept from it
by stumbling
tumbling where the face
of someone like
a swollen clown
steps forth

whose fat cheeks grow
enormous while his body
shrinks   until he stands
before us like a tiny
naked man who neither
thinks nor dreams

when in the morning sun
his face escapes him
in the empty mirror
he must ask the sky
to bring it back to him
hapless to find his way

the rage inside him
slides into his mouth
from which he vomits
words & empty sounds
his name the only
meme he knows

he is the cockeyed boss
the president of desolation
chin thrust forward
arms akimbo
legs astride
the world his carousel

a body without shape
that shrinks
& drives his mind out
through his eyes

whose teeth still clatter
syllables cut free

with this the world
will end & time
return to endless space
not to be counted
past what the fabled
start was

& the end to come

3/
while down to earth
a fool sits
on the throne
a king
by his own counting
wrapped in gold

the ground beneath him
also gold
the buckle on his belt
even the belt itself
the buttons on his shirt
all gold

gold is his heart
the rumble in his gut
gold's essence
blowing golden farts

& on his golden briefs
a stain of gold

for which all women
flock to him
all men bow down
his ring is gold
& held against your cheek
leaves gold behind

not truly gold
but close enough
to make his suitors pause
his dross
turned golden
in their sight

how loyal
little men become
losing all thought
of sacrifice
& ardor
for the common good

4/
in acts of
cruelty
the past
comes back
to life

never more true
than when
he wages
war against
the sky

the door to heaven
opens   closes
at his touch
fat angels
crowd around him

some adhering
to his flesh
the burning babes
in fancy dreams of
god & power

with an eye
that turns
from those below
his notice
or regard

the world
his mirror
fragile hands
hiding his face
& eyes

too safely blind
he will not
see you now

or me
outside his dreams

he stalks
his shadow &
his only love
the voice returning
when he dies

5/
only to call
his name out
to the world
at large

he trumpets it
until his tongue
can bear no more

the lump inside
his throat
grows daily
like a broken pump

it coughs up
clots of mud,
cold clumps

adhering
to his flesh
his plump hands
pushing them aside

like vagrant
babes swarming
around him

drunk on visions
of himself
he sucks them up
& down his maw

then out
his rump until
he dumps them

soundless
on the ground
the clown of cruelty

mad fantasist
& empty vessel
blind as any
fool

6/
deeper down
the hole
he digs for us
by digging *   * dealing

pit where pity
drops away
letting the dead
stay dead

or raising
images
too cruel
by far

the scorn
a frail man
spews
into the air

until the world
around him
bursts with voices
calling back

repeating
endlessly the words
he shows them
trolling

finding the hidden
hole his fingers
fat & swollen
open in his mouth

then raises
one frail arm
in feigned
salute

7/
Variation & Coda

he is alone the star & actor in the *farce* of history
for which an *age* waits to be named & fashioned
the fearful *price* the others pay for it

lost in his *mind* before its shadow finds our own
those *minds* that dwell in darkness that conceals his own
somehow to leave a *gap* in space & time unhealed

the *madness* lies in singularity for one & all
not in a *dream* alone but entering the world he runs from
more real than what his face sees from its mirror

his is a world in which a *fat* clown reigns
with *cheeks* the size of basketballs
a *body* racing against time to keep him whole

there is a place to raise his arms & touch the *sun*
to let his *rage* loose on the little men who mind him
cockeyed *boss* of desolation of a world gone dry

a *world* not open to the test of truth or time
until all *shape* & circumstance are lost
without a hint of where it came from or will *end*

he lives his life on *earth* apart from earth
except the way his feet search for the *ground* beneath
hoping its stones will turn to *gold* & praise him

that the earth will bring him *women* & a throne
to sleep on *gold* beds where the light turns gold
his *loyal* minions cloaking him in gold

his *cruelty* becomes his truest act of love
more *true* the more a lie conceals it
ordained from *heaven* where nightly his spirit flies

no longer bound by *flesh* grown hard or soft
his is an *eye* all-seeing like a god's a poet's eye
reflected & refracted in his *mirror* bent to please his sight

before it leaves him *blind,* a fool or beggar like the rest,
shunning the shit-*hole* worlds of prisoners & slaves,
immured from *pity* & the loser's game

the way the *images* rise up inside him
the voices in his head that *scorn* him till he cries
the *world* a prison from which escape is lost

he can only pray to catch the *words* he can't remember
to let his *fingers* trace their outlines in the dust
moving his *arm* up high to reach his mouth

his minions pining hugely for his last *salute*

A ROUND OF SOLIPSISMS
for my 86th birthday

"He takes a book down from his shelf & scribbles across a page of text: *I am the final one.* This means the world will end when he does." (from *A Paradise of Poets*)

1/
the lie of consciousness
assails me   waking
in the early hours

shorn of dreams
the world reduced to what
cannot be told

& scarce remembered
I am walking
mean-legged

toward a patch of forest
then a tunnel
where a train runs

from my sight
heading for a depot
I will never reach

2/
what is a dream
& where is it located?

when it ends
a blackness
fills the place called mind

unseen   unheard
there is no world then
& no mind to tell us

searching for a name
the word is *solipsism*

what the man
almost a corpse
knows, dying

that the world will end
when he does

3/
the real a lie
as well
(the man thinks)

struggling
to hold on
& falling back

he grabs for it
fearing as he does
its vanishing

the world without him
is no world
the stars no stars

the plot of land
under his foot
has no solidity

the water leaves
no water
& the air no air

when the imagination
fades   the fancy
takes its place

when all are gone
the mind shuts down
with scarce a trace

4/
for David Antin

you have died
& still
the world goes on

the strangeness
felt by us
without you

where I train
my thoughts
on all I know

& knowing
that for you
the world has fled

as it will flee
for me & all
the others

when the mind shuts
& the world
unthought

shuts with it

5/
the bloom of life
assaults me
when I fall
under its spell

happy to play
time's fool
like other men
before me

wisdom is a lie
only the dead
can see through
& reject

the present
never there
the past
a trick of mind

how many worlds
we hold inside us
something to be shared
until it ends

6/
inside the only
world I know
the power rests
with me

the flow of light
opens in images
& ends
in darkness

I try to find you
& the others
hearing my name re-echo
in another tongue

no one can know
or wrest from me
something I carry
until the fire starts

its hidden name
apocalypse
intended for me
alone

7/
An Exhortation –
for the Survivors

"how can there be
a world
without you?"

lightly asked
& wanting
nothing less

the years once lived
stay in the mind
only in bits

predict an image
not yet real
the hope of juncture

a contingency
foretold & closed
shutting us off

but different
when we come together
in your eyes

distant like mine
& knowing
that the end will come

to me
to you
the greater world

gone in a wink
& done
absent all care

THREE POEMS AFTER IMAGES
BY NANCY TOBIN

WAITING FOR SEURAT

waiting for seurat
is not so bad is not

what everybody thinks of
standing in a fish tank

arms akimbo legs too
when the bathers fail to make

the morning's exercise
forsaken all awash

as I am too
but now

the final holiday draws nigh
some sunday afternoon

the chime has chimed
the branches overhang

the crowd of watchers
& it's time

to coax the children
back into the car

to leave the dishes
& the soap behind

the other little friends
so soon departed

still we wait for them
we are the walkers

in the park
& if we fall into the lake

a second time
the acrobats will scoop us out

will whisk us home
like children

neither lost nor found
our bodies & our thoughts

like tiny flecks
& little reckoning

the time it takes
to sink or swim

still bug eyed
half alive

the big bowl broken
waiting for seurat

DYSTOPIA PARKWAY

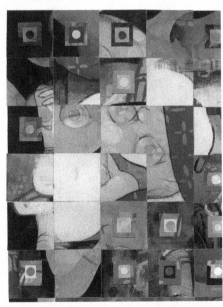

how far he dives
into a sandbox
lights erupting flicker

down a parkway
riding to the Star Hotel
a place to watch

the stars on carpets
sidewalks stitched into a
pure dystopia

as one by one
we dance
for all the children

in the world
my temper will ignite
feed you my flames

a red confusion
opens to the right of us
we raise white fingers

stubby arms
a forest of computer
screens alight

the parkway filled with
phantom windows mothers
can stare out from

their dystopias
more like a fact of life
seeing that nothing

can cohere however
solid are the walls
however bright

soap bubbles floating
over broken glass
the perch deserted where

birds seldom sang
the parkway packed into
a sun box flat

I carry underneath
my coat the memory of where
we all will live

a family of artists
each one with a simple story
resolved to bring it home

THE BEST THING
ABOUT SUNDAY

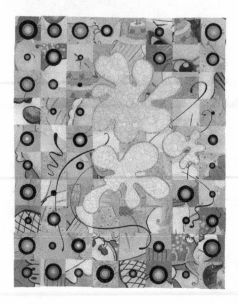

is the color
& the next best
how the little folk
find here a place to fly

balloons & kites
skidaddle
rummage among the broken
mother boards

how pink & paper thin
the world appears
to be a field of pinwheels
driven by the wind

& spinning
line on line
& circle into circle
strings cut free

these are the gifts
they bring us these
are what we throw
into the air & see them

flying by
the children's room
a little brighter
walking cockeyed looking

for the wind to stop
then we can find
the best thing about sunday
eggs & eyes

adornments cars that run
on spirits wheels
too precious for the road
a pig that squeals

NOTE. The initiatory act here follows from Nancy Tobin's quasi-abstract images and her assessment of the mysteries and revelations that her art provides her. The work as such was commissioned as a "visual word collaboration" for an exhibition at the Center for the Performing Arts, Hoboken, NJ, in May 2006.

FIVE BOOKS

BOOK ONE: A BOOK OF SHADOWS

1/
History is over.
In another world
you find another
young as you,
your shadow
over his, the two
together, sharing
hidden sorrows,
thoughts of   (G. de Nerval)
expiation. The world
does not forgive.

2/
Allotments.
Shut.
The neighbors cross the boulevard
in pairs.
The door adjacent to
our thoughts   shut also.
Therefore they shift
their legs between
short bursts,
the cadence of a march,
old world, old
fashioned melodies
unheard. A single hand
can sweep the board.

A single eye can glimpse
a shadow of the cosmos
through a pin hole.

3/
It was always dark.
The red hole's
wetness threatened
the lost sheep.
Sharp exchanges
were not clearly heard.
Rivers did
not flow.
You did not defend
your brother.
We ascend
toward progress.
I scratch fire &
remove it from your throat.
I run out of
distant shadows
now that no one
tries to stop
the passage from a city
that is drowning.

4/
I look for lights
under my fingers.
I will take them & will make
foolish minds wise.
Then when I flick my half closed eyes
your mouth will open wide

& I will sail by with my flags.
You will applaud me
when I scratch for cash
under your shadows.
I who am geared to tear down
what you build
your houses like your ashes
swept away.

5/
Poetry is made in bed
for some   for me
the call of life is stronger.
I walk & see my shadow
hanging upside down
with yours. The way
your mouth says *I*
is just like mine.
I multiply
the little portion
that your fingers
spill.

6/
I is an other   gaunt
& somewhat turned
into the light.
I threatens to return,
is hungry now
for power
as for love.
He is my own, becomes
my shadow

dog.
I reach a hand to him
& freeze.
I cannot speak
without him
though we try.

7/
I run from shadows
to avoid old people
maddened by God.
I follow animals
whose eyes at night
mirror my face.
Seeing myself asleep
I touch my arm.
I celebrate
new forms of sex.
I am frantic
knowing that nobody
has a way out
or a face
more marked than
mine.
*I was not
born live.*

(J. Holzer)

8/
It is a shame to watch
my face   to see it
running through your hands
like jelly.

I am my own
dark friend
a shadow set against
a darker shadow.
I hear a sound
like pianos
buried in the earth.
The pressure of my feet
against the pedals
opens a flood.
A carrousel is bobbing
up & down.
The happy singer
enters paradise
with seven others.

9/
There are some who shadow us
for what we love.
Nightly the passengers
still blind me
while I bind their wounds.
I feel their final jabs
between the covers & the sea
no time for preening.
I watch my feet move
among the stars.
Everything we offer
to the world
is what the world gives back
without a thought
or breath.

Coda to *A Book of Shadows*

What is remembered
of the dead is how
they tottered, little more
to write, & less
to pass a test
at understanding.
How discreet
to dance here in a hall
of shadows,
or to sit this moment,
dozing in the fast train,
while the clouds
take shape, even
as they leave
their shadows, like the dead
across the fields.
        I am more alive
for thinking of them,
knowing that the time
draws nigh,
the outline disappears,
& dark as Monday
I am marching
with the fathers, ready
to mark my presence
in their ranks.

BOOK TWO: A BOOK OF DEATHS
for David Meltzer

1/
A man without a face
is still a man.
He is the victim
of his own
worst thoughts.
The light runs from his eye.
Robbed of its speed
it blinds him.
Every moment
is the last
before death ends it.

2/
I spend long nights
in mausoleums
like a prince.
When I bite the flesh
over my thumb
it bleeds.
I lost my fear of death
last summer
& I want to teach the trick
to all my friends.

3/
A visitor
from outer space
tries hard
to summon us.

Someone says
EAT DEATH.
I fish around for answers
but the questions
still won't come.

4/
The tips of your fingers
find weather
or hide in the cave
of your glove.
You pull back
when it hurts
enhancing the pleasure.
Conception follows
or death.
Then we run away
fearful of time

5/
I will not save the world.
The power in my blood
runs through my shoe.
I have never known fatigue
but know it now. I whistle
& the dog sits still
& ponders.
Nobody else is resting
or in love.
The taste of death is in my mouth.
I suck it like an arm
until it breaks me.

6/
I put down
anyone
who tries to
put me down.
I ruminate
a proper way
to let time pass.
I take from others
what they need
& watch their deaths
leap naked
from their eyes.
I sit where space
is tightest.

7/
I baptize you
for centuries of
centuries
& watch you flail.
You wrestle me
to death.
I see a pair of you
as high as
any house.
In less time
than it takes
to stumble
I am where you dropped me.

(M. Wittig)

8/

I have no qualms
but live with satisfaction
deep in sleep.
Beware of fallen lines
the sign says:
Death along the tracks
among the lost.
I aim a spell at someone
for a price. The word *botanica*
is crystal clear.
It bothers me to be here
babbling   lonesome
every time it rains.

9/

I declare myself
the master spirit
eager to be splayed.
I run & prattle.
I will not be moved.
How much it pains me
to be last or least.
I tear dark letters
from a page &
wear them
on my skin.
The miracle of death
is only
that it sets us free.

10/

I vent my wrath
on animals
pretending they will turn
divine.
I open up
rare certainties
that test free
will.
I take from animals
a place in which
the taste of death
pours from their mouths
& drowns them.

Coda to *A Book of Deaths*

for Marcel Henaff

not hasty
or in love
with what's
to come
he sits & waits
or I do
for him
figuring the time
elapsed
the century
almost his own
& also mine
we register
the names
of those
who died

before us
their faces
lost to time
or to the failing
mind
& every day
death rides
the world
the good & bad
together
under death's sway
death's way
no grace
where light
hurts
falling on
the bodies
blown apart
the babes who died
before us
nothing hidden
left to hide
the innocent
that death
knows best
no grace
delivered by a king
the universe
receding further
from our reach
indifferent
to the way
we live & die

BOOK THREE: A BOOK OF GODS

1/
Here where god is light
a brown globe
hangs above
a burning hell.
Eyes turn right.
Hieronymus (my namesake)
let me lift this picture
from your hands.
I cherish walking in your circles.
Do you think the light is wet?
Forget it little father
& go home.
Return the keys to management.
When someone asks
if you believe in god
turn cautious.
There are now angels everywhere.
Never look back.

2/
God of the universe
manqué
you issue from my mouth.
I watch you dying.
Muscles like flowers gather
at your throat.
You shake a wrist at me.
Your watchband comes apart
& freezes.
I can see you with a babe

propped on your lap
or else a lamb.
Old man with blisters
working against time
you plunge a knife
into my book.
The babe limp as a doll
tilts forward
gagging.

3/
When we do one plus two
the light sparks up
inside its box
& what we take from it
is an adjustment.
Here I force the water through
to flush their voices.
I make a hole down which
a foot slides
severed from its shoe.
I blow the air away
until the mirror
shows me your other face.
I call the gods to witness
& when they do
I let them die.

4/
I believe in the magic of god   (J. de Lima)
& in fire. Somebody
dangles a key on the steps.
From a hole in my chest

eyes stare out.
I run into a circle
of friends
little men with pale lips
& soft fingers.
I signal new forms of expression.
The way sand shapes hills
& water shapes fountains.
I am in their hands completely
helpless as a babe
unless the babe command the world
sending a stream of
feathers
back to earth.

5/
I set loose stones
in motion
one atop
the next.
I wonder
why one thief
hangs
backwards.
The mist of morning
makes the scene
look blue.
From sleep I beckon.
While you stand in place
I race ahead.
I call on history
the way some call
on God.

What was begun
in anger
now brings peace.

6/
i is a womb
a belly
something stolen
heart & hand.
i eats
& will be eaten.
i is a habitation.
i is go & good.
i is a power.
i is to God
a question.
i is willing.
i is i-am
but stands confused.
i is a name for ice.
i is an end.

7/
I kiss every
phallus   (Takahashi M.)
hoping to find
God.
I draw a needle
through my flesh
& holler.
When the clocks run down
I meet my true love.
Someone sits here

in the dark
& cuts her toenails.
The bride of Hitler
is she not
a happy dear?
I let her ride me
like a dog.

8/
I parade for God.
I pull a tree out by the roots
uncovering a mountain.
I roll a truck
over a trail of tears
then land it in
a chuckhole.
You are near to me
& hear
the blood course through
my veins.
I raise a post & force it
deep into the soil.
There is a smell like tar
that swells my throat
a cavalcade of men at work
& grunting.

9/
I kicked a stone &
heard the voice
of God.
The pain ran
from my leg

to where
the body splits.
I called my fingers
crucibles.
The soggy smell of dirt,
the open sores,
gave little comfort.
I had kept my steps
abreast of theirs,
then turned &
cantered, closer
to their lights
in frozen motion.

10/
I dwell among you &
I dish out dreams.
I am a little god
who brays
on impulse.
Do not hesitate to call.
Your smallest wish
is sacred to me.
Sacred too is how
I ride you, spurs
into your sides.
We have no mothers
only cows
no fathers but the wind.

11/
I think of God
when fucking.
Is it wrong to pray
without a hat
to reject the call
to grace? I long to flatter
presidents & kings.
I long for manna.
I will be the first
to sail for home
the last to flaunt
my longings.
I will undo my garments.
& stand before you
naked. In winter
I will curse their god
& die.

12/
What I sniff
is eglantine
the vapors of
which god?
I dine & rest
no closer to the truth
than yesterday.
The table sags
under the burden of
a living heart.
Birds drown in flight.
I make a replica
& stitch it

to my chest.
I stare into the god's
eyes & see only
flecks of light.

13/
I am that I am
the god trills.
(He is no more a god
than I or you.)
We see his little boats
ride to the shore
& watch our fathers
like our children
muscle through the waves.
There is a cry
like anybody's
in my throat.
There is a crowd
that fails to see
how our flesh flakes off.
All eyes discern me
where I fall.

Coda for Two Voices to A Book of Gods

The grace of god
half blinds me,
half still alive,
& cries
seeing the days foretold,
the book before us,
open shut & done.

I will live on what
the god lives,
opening my mouth
to take it in
& shitting words.
The victims lie
beside me.

A deeper image
leaves the world behind,
still deeper
where time ends
& yet another universe
begins
absent all seeing.

Is the grace
a story told
or only whispered,
hard to know
here where the bodies
wait   the night
draws nigh?

The cruelty of god
is better known,
the brutal monarchy
against whose rule
we raise a new
republic
sufferance left behind

leaving the mind
a thankful blank
privileged to escape
the blasts of privilege,
we flaunt our awkwardness
the little we have to show
tackling the void

BOOK FOUR: A BOOK OF DREAMS

for Robert Kelly

1/

The way her knee swells
& she feels it
swelling & it turns into
a babe's head.
No one has a countenance
more rich
& no one has a mouth
that opens wider,
lets a sound like
dreaming come into
the room in which
they wait.

2/

In the night
men go fishing for stars,
not a god but a babe
wields the trident.
Cables lie covered with
smut. Light erupts

on a screen. What you see
is your face   & the face
that you see, old
& blind,
is a face from
your dreams.

3/
Better for the mind
to empty out
in dreams,
the way a body
falls, thrown
from a passing train,
forsaken.
They hold a plate
between them, on its rim
a graven message:
GOD IS PAIN.

4/
The air has grown destructive,
finds a way
to bind you,
fat & swollen,
an old angel with
flayed wings
The searchers in the night
drift past you.
You will walk among them,
will give them solace,
only in your dreams.

5/

The room in which the man
is sleeping
splinters   halfway
through his dream
he feels a flow
of images escaping
from his eyes
imploding coating
bed & floor
with colors like a show
of lights
in space, a spectrum
half unseen,
unsought.

6/

Gardens blossom where a hand
digs deep   the rows
of laborers,
small men forgotten
like the names of towns,
bend with the wind.
Bright words like *bella*
grace their dreams,
their days degraded by
inane *lavoro*.
Theirs are forbidden thoughts.

7/

Hand in hand
the dead walk in a line,
hoping against hope,

like children.
It is enough. It
is enough.
It doesn't last.
The false commanders
lead the charge.
The story, started
in a dream,
is winding down.

8/
French dolls like ghosts
step forth at midday.
Everyone is *sportif*
geared for speed
never to turn a shoulder,
to name a game for love.
Their aim is circular,
it follows where you lead them,
down a secret path,
into a basement
shadowed by
your childhood dream,
a lurking hole,
then up the backstairs
lost to sleep.

9/
In the dark dance,
sightless,
they are tearing at a bone,
their jaws like bears'
jaws   cavernous

their fingers dripping
porridge, clawing
at each other's nipples,
keepers of a dream.
The blind man sees
no flame or smoke
but knows it all
by tasting.

10/
The cavern of the universe
widens each morning.
My head fills up with dew,
the father writes,
having no home but where
his shadow leads him.
In greasy shirtsleeves, heavy
lids, blotched faces,
the men pursue
a trail of tears,
unbuttoned   captive
to a dream,
a starless galaxy,
the deeper sky
a field of images
measureless & mindless,
absent their god.

11/
The man with a hole
in his eye
sees anew. A sphinx
fingers a sphincter,

she extrudes
false colors. The night
once was pink,
it is now
black & white.
Nerval in a corner
spitting his death out,
a substance
first dreamed,
then stuck under
his tongue.
The war goes on forever.

12/
"Release me."
"Feed me."
Whose design this is
they do not know,
but cling to cyberspace
as if it held
a clue   the outline
of a village
filled with snow
or circumstance.
The wise man runs from it,
like poetry
or dreams.

13/
Love, like intelligence,
opens a door,
to let us in
still blind

& searching,
taking as a sign
the names of God
engraved in
amethyst   a counterfeit
infinity,
not letting time
pretend to halt
the darker flux,
impediment to where
we set our sights.
Here is a place to hang
a flag, and there a hat
to pull a flag from.
All your little men
are watching,
waking from a dream.
There is no predicting
summer
but it always comes.

14/
Those who are masters
needn't talk,
but signal with a secret
nod or wink,
concealed assassins
brought into the mix.
Involuntary tears,
a dream of executions,
smoke
rises between our teeth.
The ones who loved us

(C. Baudelaire)

die   not one by one
but now *en masse,*
the presence of the dead
in every corner.

15/
Inside the house,
its walls down,
ground into a dust
that only the dream
sustains, those
who were once alive
do not arise,
but *one by one*
by snakes   (T.L. Beddoes)
their limbs are swallowed.
Almost enough
to make you
suffocate, to lodge
like mercury
under your tongue.

16/
Our dreams were of suns,
of vermilion dragons
spangled with gold
from Sumeria,
pronouncements & omens
concealed, to take death
as a tribute,
a slave plunged
in water
& drowning,

becoming a wife
to their god,
a scorpion,
then a chimera.

Coda to *A Book of Dreams*

> *O God, I could be bounded in a nutshell and count my-*
> *self a king of infinite space, were it not that I have bad*
> *dreams.*

No world more clear
than what we see
in dreams
nor more amazing,
numbers bursting into
stars   & stars
enriching what we learn
when dreaming.

It is no more than this,
to sleep & be
the master of the universe,
not to be bound to earth
but gathering a trillion
other worlds,
to count myself
a little king
stepping aside for time.

Nothing is measured
that the mind can fathom
waking. In the way
your body beckons
when I turn to touch you
coming from a black hole
deep in space
& time   I learn to count
the deeper images
& those still deeper,
gods & angels
dancing on a pin. *   * a chip

Before the dream
turns bad
in which a pin* holds   * a chip
all we know
& all we fear
I stretch out flat
to the Horizon.
I arch above you
like a lid.
I vanish & return.
My name is Death.

The word *extermination*
resonates   nothing
escapes. The world
itself ends in a time
beyond all time
where time ends
leaving a residue behind
of mindless space

& still more mindless
images   the nightmares
that the mind conceals.*   * reveals

To run from time
isn't a choice,
the stars we see
are overwhelming
& block the view
or bring up images
of light & dark,
a flickering
across the map
of time,
the flow of sand
in dreams.

BOOK FIVE: A BOOK OF MIRRORS

1/
I smile into a mirror
& my face
glares back.
A father holds his babe
up to the light.
Where will it lead us?
Heaven is no place for fools.
I run my fingers
through your hair
& feel the universe
shut down.

2/
The generals are gathering.
They stare into each other's eyes
through mirrors.
With a display of wounds
we signal them
& turn away. I am the last
because the fire
deep inside
burns till it's morning.

3/
Great distances
are mine. I plot
their numbers
but I know
that every universe
contains another.
There is no end in sight
& no beginning.
The stars stay dark
in mirrors
until your fingers
counting them
have dropped away.

4/
We look at every mirror
as a mere memento.
Mirages have arisen
& we swim in them.
I make my way by stealth.
In a house of children

no one reigns
or sleeps. The walls
start at the floor
& touch the ceiling.

5/
Eager to break through language
& touch life
I crack my head against
a mirror.
I hack at a false body
with a stick
pushing the flames apart
until the heart appears.

6/
I find a secret world in mirrors.
My fingernails are pale,
my steps are perpendicular.
I parachute & strut.
I seek acceleration day by day.
I am a man who swims among the grifters.
Istanbul is not my home.
I turn a page & listen.
I am as hard as nails.
My body swells from all the sounds inside it.
I show myself in dreams.

7/
Separated by a cranny
others   more aware
stare down at us.
We have no way

to talk together,
mirror neurons that respond
only to themselves
& not to others.
A place to stand
deep in the speaker's mind
determines speech.
The plan is self-erasing
if we wait it out,
not one of us the worse
for wear.

8/
They were prey to
maneuverings,
played them with zeal,
to no end
that they knew,
to declare new beginnings,
bestriding a sand dune,
vacuums a god might
transform to a cosmos,
infinity's mirror,
a place internal to place,
a procedure a king
once devised,
divination from innards,
a rapturous babble.

9/
A world caught in a mirror
too vast to be contained.
Infinities of mirrors.

The ones who see it
falter, their hands
break the glass.
They are the sorry mystics,
misfits from
the middle states,
we spy them
on a distant planet,
hidden from time.

Coda to *A Book of Mirrors*

The way a face
recalls a face
by looking past it,
looking twice
when once will do.

Reflection tells it all.

There is no better way
to measure time,
the little jesters
in the field behind you
shaking loose
the small words
clicking in their craws.

All is seen,
the mirror as a field
for memory,
your own face

foremost   a receptacle
for other faces,
old & worn.

The images not deep
but multiplied,
held on a shining surface,
we can count them
as they pass
& then return.

In a room
where all the walls
are mirrors.
you are a mirror
of yourself,
a phantom child,
elliptical.

The mystery of mirrors,
counted & re-counted
ten times over.

Right is left,
the wound across
your heart
favors the rise & fall
of breath,
the top & bottom
still in place.

Therefore it turns
into a game,

something to carry
with you,
the next time
the grave comes open,
& you enter
where a floor of mirrors
waits for you
& blinds you.*   * binds you

NOTE. The first of the five "books" presented here was commissioned by Tita Reut for a series of artists' books that she was then publishing in Paris. For these and for the six "books" that followed I drew from earlier poems of mine, breaking them into fragments or stanzas containing respectively the words "shadows," "deaths," "gods," "dreams," and "mirrors," to each of which I added a newly composed coda. As a further act of retrospection and autovariation, they fit for me into the work of reclamation I was then engaged in.

THE MYSTERIES OF MIND LAID BARE
IN TALKING

in memory of David Antin

1/
I would also say it
speaking   would like to hear it
catapulting from my mouth

not like a flow of words
but a barrage of pulses
one athwart the other

mindful how some spirit
wracked you
who were singular in speech

the mysteries of mind
laid bare in talking
discovered first, then lost

the way all times
are lost   when no one
counts them off

a dream expresses it
still harder to remember
pressured to write it down

they wait a new device
a camera to record
the images in dreams

the images in memory
of days in New York
or of walks in Paris

linked in talk
& warm embraces
on the other coast

is where we come
to die   at last
the more we wander

conversant with the dead
companions all
stiff necked & lonely

when you ask me for
a discourse
still more satisfying

that our cheating hearts
hold back
then let it fly

2/
the memories
of being young
your black hair
in the wind

later to be lost
like *something*

keys hair someone
a contingency

my noble forehead
that you saw
or claimed to
in the loss of yours

the stream of language
hard to fix
or to deflect
once lost

first meetings
faces also lost
like words on paper
that we shared

carried over time
the thoughts
of sickness
shared with all

like dying
thrice denied
the distance between
now & now

I do not see you
any longer
but know the voice
full in my mind

so much like mine
someone had said
imagination all
that makes it sound

timed to my heart
that keeps the beat
flesh sundered
turned to ash

imagination
only
can it be fair
to write

a love song
to a friend

3/
from friend to friend
the voice comes
& the answer
that a stranger overhears
robs him of speech

the guest is half
oracular
nowhere he turns
or runs   caught
in a web

or caught between
two open doors

is right for him
the way out west
leads back to asia

asia leads him
into wilderness
a bitter landscape
where no friend
survives

no gaze or touch
so tender
those who fight
for love
once living

know it as a taste
sweet in the mouth
though distant
at length   at last
the friend is double

in your sight
but turns from you
the time to come
draws nigh
then shatters

& does the poem exist
when there is no one there
to hear it?

4/
who does not dream
dreams deeper
by not dreaming

until the door
swings open
draws you to
sleep within

what forms
assailing us
the scattered dreamers

curtains closing
on our eyes
in frantic bursts
lights streaming

take the shape
of birds & stars
outlyers

move across the sky
the eye in love
with tentacles
in mauve & amber

the new year
underway
without you

then the rest
is dream
whether the images
arise or not

the screen goes blank
foretold by you
the dreamer

here is the death
we feared
infinite space
to every side

absent all light

5/
AFTER WANG WEI

> *O my friends! there is no friend.*

at Weiching
       morning rain
              the fine dust damped
a guest house
       green among
              green willows
urge a friend
       to drink a final
              glass of wine
west of Yang Pass
       there is
              no friend

6/
THE MAKING OF A DREAM

except the memory
the loss   a dream
that will not stick
but comes & goes
as if we hadn't
dreamed it

for which I name you
poet of the dream
in whose denial
dreams come forth
the word "desire"
foremost

pleasures first
a place as large
as Prospect Park
where others
feast & bathe
some sleeping

& the dreamer
kicks his shoes off
wades into a pool
the north branch of
an old estate
its master far away

then goes from room
to room in search
of shoes   as prelude
to a silent movie
buried like his life
too deep for tears

for which the word
the woman
throws at him
is *hog* (he says)
not out of shame
or fecklessness

but turning
subject into object
echoing the master's
words   *the world*
is everything
that is the case

waking & dreaming
much the same

NOTE. The dream covered lightly in the final section, above, is from David
Antin's "On Narrative: The Beggar and the King," published previously (2010)
in my blog/magazine *Poems and Poetics (Jacket2)*. The full poem as it appears
here was published February 1, 2017 on what would have been his 85th
birthday.

POST-FACE

The title of the present gathering — like much of what I've written over the years — points to the time through which we're now living and to the times before through which I've also lived. The sense of desolation and devastation — a sadly rhyming pair — continues to inform our lives as vulnerable beings, both politically and ecologically, and it enters into our words and thoughts as poets in what Pablo Neruda famously titled our (all too bounded) "residence on earth." To all of this I am a witness, or, better put, the poems bear witness on my behalf, even where the writing is procedural or seeming to put process over substance — & maybe especially then. In composing this book I've inserted some accounts concerning form & occasion, but my sense of the life & politics outside the book come across more directly in the following excerpt from an interview recently conducted for Spanish publication by the Mexican poet Javier Taboada.

I would like to link one of your poems, Twentieth Century Unlimited, *with the outcome of the presidential elections (2016) in the United States:*

> *As the twentieth century fades out*
> *the nineteenth begins*
> > *again*
> *it is as if nothing happened*
> *though those who lived it thought*
> *that everything was happening*
> *enough to name a world for & a time*
> *to hold it in your hand*
> *unlimited   the last delusion*
> *like the perfect mask of death*

Do you think that the 'last delusion' has already been unmasked?

The poem goes back to the 1990s when the Cold War was coming to an end and with it — for better or worse — many of the twentieth-century dreams of human perfectibility and unlimited progress that we had taken too easily for granted. That was the "last delusion" I was talking about then, but the still darker thrust of the poem was the sense, already forming, of a retrogression to precisely the conditions that those dreams and delusions were aiming to address. We were moving, in other words, into a new century and millennium, but what was emerging already was a return to the conditions of the century before: "nationalism, colonialism and imperialism, ethnic and religious violence, growing extremes of wealth and poverty" in the description Jeffrey Robinson and I provided for the pre-face to the third volume of *Poems for the Millennium*. To which we added: "All reemerge today with a virulence that calls up their earlier nineteenth-century versions and all the physical and mental struggles against them, struggles in which poetry and poets took a sometimes central part."

This wasn't prophecy (though it might have been) but my sense of history speaking and unfolding for us in the here and now. And it has only intensified over the last two decades: the *farce* that history has now become in Trump's time, but not without the threat of *tragedy* as well. To speak more specifically, what's marking the present century — whether it resembles the nineteenth or not — are two distinct emergences: the rise of ISIS-like religious movements over the last two decades (and not only Muslim) and the rise of the nationalism and jingoism that Trump is bringing to us in the United States, and others like him elsewhere. Not to equate the two too easily, both are threats to a fact-based sense of reality on the one hand and to an open life of the imagination on the other, and my own push, like that of most poets I know, is to bring the two together: "imaginary gardens with real toads in them," as Marianne Moore once had it.

So yes, I think the mask has already fallen off and we again have to take account of the actual present that confronts and threatens us. For this, poetry would be my own immediate answer, as it has always been, but there are other answers as well — and maybe, in the short run, better. Under any circumstances, the threats of violence and closure are what we have to stand against — wherever found and however answered.

Those anyway are the deeper thoughts ("too deep for tears") underlying the bulk of my present writings, and I thought it useful to call attention to them here

Is this what you meant when in A Further Witness *you wrote: "the age of the assassins/ once deferred/ comes back/ full blast"? Where do you think all this will lead?*

At my age I'm suddenly feeling closed off from a future that I'm not likely to see, but I can try to answer the question as if I'll be a part of it. With that in mind I can reconstruct fairly easily what I was getting at in *A Further Witness*: the sense of terrorism (also a tactic with nineteenth-century roots) as a notable and distressing fact of our new and present reality. By assassination, then, I mean murder as a public and political act, not only aimed at rulers and leaders but, very much so, at the world-at-large. I could have also said the age of the murderers but I think that "age of the assassins" carries an echo for me and others of something from Rimbaud (*Voici le temps des Assassins*); at least that was the way I used it here. And there was also the other word that kept coming into the poetry — *cruelty* — as a signal of what we had to fear in the world that we knew from before and that kept coming back no matter how much we tried to defer it. As much as I feared and hated it, whether active or passive, I knew it was something that had to be right there, at the core of what I thought and wrote as a poet. It is for this reason that I used it several times as a book title, *A Cruel Nirvana,* in English, French, and Spanish, and in a poem of that name, which ends with these lines:

It is summer
but the trees
are dead.
They vanish with
our fallen friends.
The eye in torment
brings them down
each mind a little world
a cruel nirvana.

That would put it even at the heart of religious or spiritual attempts to escape it — the cruelty of the escape from cruelty — but its most hideous effects are in the public world and in the murders and tortures that serve as instruments of policy or, worse yet, of belief. So the idea, much needed today, is not to exclude it but to bring it into the body of the poem, as a sign of both the terror and the pity that the poem calls forth.

Jerome Rothenberg, internationally known poet/translator/ editor/essayist, is the author of more than eighty volumes of published poetry, a dozen important books of translations, and ten groundbreaking anthologies of contemporary and traditional poetry, including *Technicians of the Sacred* and, with Pierre Joris and Jeffrey C. Robinson, *Poems for the Millennium* in five volumes.

TITLES FROM BLACK WIDOW PRESS
TRANSLATION SERIES

A Life of Poems, Poems of a Life by Anna de Noailles. Translated by Norman R. Shapiro. Introduction by Catherine Perry.

Approximate Man and Other Writings by Tristan Tzara. Translated and edited by Mary Ann Caws.

Art Poétique by Guillevic. Translated by Maureen Smith.

The Big Game by Benjamin Péret. Translated with an introduction by Marilyn Kallet.

Boris Vian Invents Boris Vian: A Boris Vian Reader. Edited and translated by Julia Older.

Capital of Pain by Paul Eluard. Translated by Mary Ann Caws, Patricia Terry, and Nancy Kline.

Chanson Dada: Selected Poems by Tristan Tzara. Translated with an introduction and essay by Lee Harwood.

Earthlight (Clair de Terre) by André Breton. Translated by Bill Zavatsky and Zack Rogow. (New and revised edition.)

Essential Poems and Prose of Jules Laforgue. Translated and edited by Patricia Terry.

Essential Poems and Writings of Joyce Mansour: A Bilingual Anthology. Translated with an introduction by Serge Gavronsky.

Essential Poems and Writings of Robert Desnos: A Bilingual Anthology. Edited with an introduction and essay by Mary Ann Caws.

EyeSeas (Les Ziaux) by Raymond Queneau. Translated with an introduction by Daniela Hurezanu and Stephen Kessler.

Fables in a Modern Key by Pierre Coran. Translated by Norman R. Shapiro. Full-color illustrations by Olga Pastuchiv.

Fables of Town & Country by Pierre Coran. Translated by Norman R. Shapiro. Full-color illustrations by Olga Pastuchiv.

Forbidden Pleasures: New Selected Poems 1924–1949 by Luis Cernuda. Translated by Stephen Kessler.

Furor and Mystery & Other Writings by René Char. Translated by Mary Ann Caws and Nancy Kline.

The Gentle Genius of Cécile Périn: Selected Poems (1906–1956). Edited and translated by Norman R. Shapiro.

Guarding the Air: Selected Poems of Gunnar Harding. Translated and edited by Roger Greenwald.

Howls & Growls: French Poems to Bark By. Translated by Norman R. Shapiro; illustrated by Olga K. Pastuchiv. *(forthcoming)*

I Have Invented Nothing: Selected Poems by Jean-Pierre Rosnay. Translated by J. Kates.

The Inventor of Love & Other Writings by Gherasim Luca. Translated by Julian & Laura Semilian. Introduction by Andrei Codrescu. Essay by Petre Răileanu.

Jules Supervielle: Selected Prose and Poetry. Translated by Nancy Kline & Patricia Terry.

La Fontaine's Bawdy by Jean de La Fontaine. Translated with an introduction by Norman R. Shapiro.

Last Love Poems of Paul Eluard. Translated with an introduction by Marilyn Kallet.

Love, Poetry (L'amour la poésie) by Paul Eluard. Translated with an essay by Stuart Kendall.

Pierre Reverdy: Poems, Early to Late. Translated by Mary Ann Caws and Patricia Terry.

Poems of André Breton: A Bilingual Anthology. Translated with essays by Jean-Pierre Cauvin and Mary Ann Caws.

Poems of A.O. Barnabooth by Valery Larbaud. Translated by Ron Padgett and Bill Zavatsky.

Poems of Consummation by Vicente Aleixandre. Translated by Stephen Kessler.

Préversities: A Jacques Prévert Sampler. Translated and edited by Norman R. Shapiro.

RhymeAmusings (AmuseRimes) by Pierre Coran. Translated by Norman R. Shapiro. *(forthcoming)*

The Sea and Other Poems by Guillevic. Translated by Patricia Terry. Introduction by Monique Chefdor.

Through Naked Branches by Tarjei Vesaas. Translated, edited, and introduced by Roger Greenwald.

To Speak, to Tell You? Poems by Sabine Sicaud. Translated by Norman R. Shapiro. Introduction and notes by Odile Ayral-Clause.

MODERN POETRY SERIES

BARNSTONE, WILLIS.
ABC of Translation

BRINKS, DAVE.
The Caveat Onus
The Secret Brain: Selected Poems 1995–2012

CESEREANU, RUXANDRA.
Crusader-Woman. Translated by Adam J. Sorkin.
    Introduction by Andrei Codrescu.
Forgiven Submarine by Ruxandra Cesereanu
    and Andrei Codrescu.

ESHLEMAN, CLAYTON.
An Alchemist with One Eye on Fire
Anticline
Archaic Design
Clayton Eshleman/The Essential Poetry: 1960–2015
Grindstone of Rapport: A Clayton Eshleman Reader
Penetralia
Pollen Aria **(forthcoming)**
The Price of Experience
Curdled Skulls: Poems of Bernard Bador. Translated
    by Bernard Bador with Clayton Eshleman.
Endure: Poems by Bei Dao. Translated by
    Clayton Eshleman and Lucas Klein.

JORIS, PIERRE.
Barzakh (Poems 2000–2012)
Exile Is My Trade: A Habib Tengour Reader

KALLET, MARILYN.
How Our Bodies Learned
The Love That Moves Me
Packing Light: New and Selected Poems
Disenchanted City (La ville désenchantée)
    by Chantal Bizzini. Translated by J. Bradford
    Anderson, Darren Jackson, and Marilyn Kallet.

KELLY, ROBERT.
Fire Exit
The Hexagon

KESSLER, STEPHEN.
Garage Elegies

LAVENDER, BILL.
Memory Wing

LEVINSON, HELLER.
from stone this running
LinguaQuake
Tenebraed
Un- **(forthcoming)**
Wrack Lariat

OLSON, JOHN.
Backscatter: New and Selected Poems
Dada Budapest
Larynx Galaxy

OSUNDARE, NIYI.
City Without People: The Katrina Poems

ROBERTSON, MEBANE.
An American Unconscious
Signal from Draco: New and Selected Poems

ROTHENBERG, JEROME.
Concealments and Caprichos
Eye of Witness: A J. Rothenberg Reader. Edited
    with commentaries by Heriberto Yepez &
    Jerome Rothenberg.
The President of Desolation & Other Poems

SAÏD, AMINA.
The Present Tense of the World: Poems 2000–2009.
    Translated with an introduction by
    Marilyn Hacker.

SHIVANI, ANIS.
Soraya (Sonnets)

WARD, JERRY W., JR.
Fractal Song

LITERARY THEORY / BIOGRAPHY SERIES

*Barbaric Vast & Wild: A Gathering of Outside and
Subterranean Poetry (Poems for the Millennium,
vol. 5).* Editors: Jerome Rothenberg and
John Bloomberg-Rissman

Clayton Eshleman: The Whole Art
by Stuart Kendall

Revolution of the Mind: The Life of André Breton
by Mark Polizzotti

WWW.BLACKWIDOWPRESS.COM

CPSIA information can be obtained
at www.ICGtesting.com
Printed in the USA
LVHW042005230623
750624LV00003B/410

9 780999 580387